DHARMA'S DANCE

poems by

Christine Poythress

Finishing Line Press
Georgetown, Kentucky

DHARMA'S DANCE

For my daughter Nicole, may you find delight in poetry.

"Trying to define yourself is like trying to bite your own teeth."
Alan Watts

Copyright © 2025 by Christine Poythress
ISBN 979-8-88838-908-9 First Edition
All rights reserved under International and Pan-American Copyright Conventions.
No part of this book may be reproduced in any manner whatsoever without written permission from the publisher, except in the case of brief quotations embodied in critical articles and reviews.

ACKNOWLEDGMENTS

My gratitude to the editors of *Quilkeepers Press,* in which "For Leonard" and "Interior Design (now "Detritus")" first appeared.

Publisher: Leah Huete de Maines
Editor: Christen Kincaid
Cover Art: Christine Poythress
Author Photo: Nora Canfield, MsDigPhotography
Cover Design: Elizabeth Maines McCleavy

Order online: www.finishinglinepress.com
also available on amazon.com

Author inquiries and mail orders:
Finishing Line Press
PO Box 1626
Georgetown, Kentucky 40324
USA

Contents

Dharma is a concept that appears in Hinduism, Jainism, Sikhism, and Buddhism. It is a combination of morality and spiritual discipline that guides how a person lives their life.

I.

THE CHASE

MADNESS

Falling in love one teeters on the edge of insanity.

Unconscious attraction
    sparks the limbic system that
        floods the pre-frontal cortex as

adrenaline
    rushes, heart races
        palms sweat.

Pheromones
    though odorless
        arouse lust.

This temporary togetherness
    soon recedes
        as bliss becomes

pedestrian and
    oxytocin cements
        companionship

or failing that
    we fall away in
        abandonment.

Ebbing hormones
    settled now
        as clear-brained

I see
    you are not
        what I believed.

MUSIC MAN

Marty, you played the flute
I sang flying 16th notes as
we performed Sir Henry Bishop
It was magic we also had a band.

Though I'd already left you, I
sang on your college senior recital.
Again the flying 16th notes. It was
1976 the last time I saw you.

In 1979, your parents
visited me in New York City
and until your father's death
they called and sent pictures.

In 2003, though you were a
runner, a massive heart attack
took your life. I always meant
to tell you how I regretted leaving.

Be kind—he's a sensitive soul,
our psychology professor had said.
Feeling unworthy, terrified, I'd fled.

Your mother forgave me
understood and loved me still.
The gash in your heart healed
you found joy fathered a son.

You were this life's true love.
Now I read your poetry prose
converse with your pictures.
All are quiet, like you were.

If there's a spirit world
a resting place of souls and
should I find you there,
I'll pray you have forgiven me.

Once we were music and I was loved.

CUP OF LOVE

Sky drunk morning glories herald the dawn
      bookends to withered moonflowers.

As I sip divine broth of coffee with sugar, cardamom and cream
      my thoughts drift to a lifetime ago

when I was young and twenty and we danced till three
      thinking it would never end.

THE GIFT

You play well, John says.
(I'd only played piano for two years.)
I thought you played as a child.

I think he's my boyfriend
me a singer dreaming of togetherness
he a pianist, composer, conductor.

Something you can play, sight read.
A handwritten, one-page composition
he gives me for my 24th birthday.

It's a slow and somber piece
whose final notes float skyward as he
drifts away in the arms of a dancer.

BRUTALLY HANDSOME

A son in the line of Judah you like King Solomon were majestic, wise, and strong, also the most handsome man I'd ever seen. Six feet tall with crystal eyes, and broad shoulders, you could have been a warrior, the king of all Zion. The melodies from your bamboo Pied Pipers flute wound around me beckoning. A naïve *papillion* who craved love I drown in your magic, my consciousness sleeping in stupor. Your dark woody scent intoxicated me and lingered for decades, a choking melancholy a gauge for each new lover. Ten years after I left California, I picked up the phone, and your voice sent a shudder through my soul. Reconnecting, I confessed I'd loved you. *Why didn't you tell me?* You never wanted children. *But people can change.* I doubted that. You suggested I come to visit you in Eureka, but I had a daughter and a steady gig. Were you lonely and just happened to think of me like the time you reappeared after dating your art professor for a year? I took you back then, but what do you want now? Your invitation, a casual utterance from 2500 miles away, was meaningless. That night I dreamed I died again in your embrace, and as I gazed into your azure eyes, my body melted into yours. But I woke to my reality. Five years later I reached out, but you responded *Do not contact me,* saying my email was spam to you. Stricken by your vitriol, I threw away the letter and picture you'd sent. Another decade passed and you found me on Facebook. Asking for friendship, you were feeling time's slippage. Had you forgotten that I was spam? No. I was your lover. I cannot be your friend. A poor girl I was not the one who *would allow you to do your art,* release you from life's labor. Now, you are only a memory, a phantom. Puff Daddy was right. "It's All About the Benjamins."

JUST A GIRL

Body blazing
       face rivaling
Helen of Troy.
       Beauty obscured
the depth of me.

To you I was
       a lonely girl
cocktail waitress
       nights in a disco
an easy mark.

To me you were
       momentary
a ride on the
       limb of love just a
passing fancy.

TEXAS TROUBADOUR

Never had I been a groupie. Not until a raven-haired son of Amarillo walked into the Palomino. His Native features and lanky stride stopped me in my tracks. A singer myself I thought we shared a bond, so I took you home. At four in the morning, you sent a new song on cassette via taxi to your manager. When I gazed into your eyes, I knew you'd be polite Texas boy, as you lied to my face sayin' it had been so long since you'd held a woman. I pulled you in if only for the night. Leaving, you took my number, but I knew you'd never call. I should've known you'd be dismissive when I saw you the next night. You'd said nothing to lead me on, but I was hoping for a second helping of cowboy wine, one more night to hold you. Will you remember me in song vague images, references to the night you slipped through my arms and for a moment I held a singer stranger, took a minstrel home, and made love beneath a cornbread moon?

PARADOX

The slip of the tongue the dart
of the dream lifted me out of the land of rednecks
racists and a small-minded life chained in marriage.
A wanna-be opera singer, country star, fitting nowhere.

I spent the '70s in California,
then New York chasing dreams and closeness.
But relationships slipped away in months
so focused was I on singing.

I landed back in Dixieland
marrying David, settling for less.
She needs more time alone than most people.
Mama knew her flower child's need for silence,
How David disturbed my soul.

But love and career can coexist.
My two favorite couples have terminal degrees.
Ph.D. psychologists a duo of champions,
two musical mentors, a Ph.D. and an Ed.D.

If music hadn't stolen my being,
psychology would've been my mistress.
After all, certifiable craziness
dances in my DNA.

PABLO

Pablo borrowed composition
overlaid it with jarring geometry.
His work bold, clever, ground shattering.

I don't love Picasso.
Waking I wouldn't wish
to see female forms torn asunder.

He told Françoise Gilot
women are machines for suffering.
For me there are only two kinds of women:
goddesses and doormats.

Misogynist, sociopath?
Yet women flocked
to his mystery.

Of another time,
I would never darken his door
nor hang his work.

But had we met
could I have torn myself
from his musk?

GO WHERE?

Now that you've got me, don't let yourself go, he said.
       "Go where?" I should have said.

I forgive you.
       I need no forgiveness.

You abandoned our marriage, our baby.
       Stayed out all night with a barfly.

              Choked me
                   left me alone
with a two-year-old.

No!
       Abide in hell
              with your demon brethren.

FOR LEONARD

My first husband who was gay and died of AIDS

Fate
impartial, cruel
devours man.

Such are the workings of the universe.

I cry
for all the Leonards
families torn bodies broken.

Fair, innocent
ravaged by disease
beauty scarred by pain.

Over half a million died the skinny death.

Your laughter, smile
fair hair, gentle eyes
we, lovers and friends

together but for biology.
Fleeting camaraderie
men we admired boys we craved.

Husband of my heart, lover of my mind.

When sick, you returned to Australia.
My last letter mailed the day and hour of your passing.
Sent back unopened June 1994.

You slipped away
lost beyond temporal existence
existing in memory.

We twin souls entwined.
You rest fly expand.
I shall meet you on the shore of eternity.

A DOG?

I sit berating
       my aloneness, mind chewing the past.

Why don't I have a lover?
       Boredom, perhaps, but I've had a hundred fleeting
pleasures.

Why don't I have a husband?
       I had four who seemed more trouble than benefit.

Bad choices—except for the gay one.
       I couldn't keep a relationship past two years.

But a human needs touch, closeness.
       At what cost?

Once I loved two dogs and twenty-three cats
       now resting in earth wooden boxes.

Yes. I want a relationship, but
       married women say they envy my freedom.

So, no, there's a price for everything.
       Maybe another dog?

II.

TWILIGHT

UNQUIET MIND

Had I at 19 missed
the starting gate?
I thought so.

At 22, bubbly college girls
younger than me with
no drugs or abortions

revered me, a Renaissance
woman—singer, painter,
piano player.

But I'd barely begun, felt like an imposter.

Images collided in my head
faster than my hands could capture them
abstract waves of violet, crimson, and ochre
flitted behind closed eyes.

Though I wrote in secret, music eclipsed art and won my heart.

Singing for decades while
sketching and dashing down
furtive poems and musings

my unquiet mind
bewitched by colors churned
with ideas, fodder for stories.

My ancient love watching my hands

carve words on paper
smear color on boards
ink flowing from the nib.

Life's fragments on page and canvas.

YOU LOOK

good for your age, you say. I am 42
running six days a week in fabulous shape.

Svelte, strong, in my sexual prime
I'm prowling for love or something like it.

And what do you offer man with wrinkled lips?
Only a backhanded compliment.

LUCITE

Electricity races up my spine as I stand in the hallway
feeling a tingle at the nape of my neck.

Is this magic murmuring in my ear a missive from the universe?
In Manhattan, Jonathan, a seven-foot-tall presence, guarded me

accompanied my nocturnal wanderings hailing last-minute taxis.
Spirit guides and last-minute taxi rides are distant memories.

I've birthed a human and am navigating single parenthood.
Still, visions explode during my waking hours as

unexpected flashes of amethyst light encircle random objects.
At night, plum-colored ribbons race beside my car.

Taking a band-aid off my six-year-old daughter's healed finger
two tubes of neon purple fly past me.

At night, a luminous object composed of triangles
spins across my bedroom, leaving trails of mauves and violets.

Is this my long-lost guardian whispering, calling me to wake up?
Or has meditating three times a day given me access to another realm?

Maybe my eyes are diseased. The ophthalmologist finds no problems.
But then, I didn't mention my personal light show.

A runner I look thirty-five skin still smooth.
But I am 43, my period erratic, practically nonexistent.

Doctor number two's diagnosis: perimenopause.
My personal summer has begun and hot flashes

the prequel to my inevitable metamorphosis have arrived.
The wise-woman staircase beckons me toward crone-hood.

Older women are often traded for younger models.
I begin questioning my sell-by date.

One evening I step into the courtyard at a city market
wraithlike, winding through the crowd brushing

past clusters of men but I feel no response.
The world has shifted, the air is static.

At 26, I'd enter a room and own the space.
You exude sexuality. Men flock to you, a boyfriend once said.

Now, as I stare down life's last stretch, my ego is freaking out.
Eventually, it won't matter how much I run.

Younger girls with tauter limbs are crowding the courtyard
and I don't smell of blood, life's perfume, the aroma of fertility.

Are my honey-dripping days over?
I'm not ready for this paradigm shift.

To men I'm a blur faded light.
Translucent, I'm walking Lucite.

2022

Each kiss of summer
sprinkles once alabaster skin
with freckles and age spots.

Long before I had need of it
Mitchum's 1964's ad proclaimed:
"Prevent horrid age spots . . ."

Yet these wisdom spots
waltz across my face,
chest, and arms.

Big sister and I
still walk the green earth.
Two septuagenarians

our boyfriends from '69
dead. Our wrinkles deepen
waistlines widen.

Expensive face creams,
a futile kindness. It's such folly
chasing youth.

SENESCENT YEARS

Firm muscle once buttressed by form
now softens as cross-hatching creeps,
etching history upon mouth, brow.

My blonde mane, once a temptress, gray
I feel 18 until rising brings
creaking bones, misty mind.

Veiny hands now cradle babies
children marvel at my roadmaps
my once full lips whose edges sag.

Youthful galloping energy
my manic madness slowed to a walk.
Without decay we like gods immortal.

Loved or feared death rears its head
and even the gift of wisdom ends in stillness.
I don't always like the inevitable.

TWILIGHT

The sun a fat ripe tomato
oozes red rivulets across the sky
and sinks, caressing the horizon.

Hazy shadows grow long.
I watch the day unwind as
twilight casts her spell.

Darkness bends her head
as night embraces trees
shrouding them in blackness

their murky shadows shading
my sallowing skin night eyes
soon heavy with sleep.

III.

SOUL SHEDDING

LAST SUNLIGHT

I should have quit sooner Mother says as we are pruning shrubs in her front
    yard.
She's 73 just retired and since Daddy died, she's worked for 15 years.

Still her witty, lively self, she volunteers at the symphony,
socializes with friends and sings in the church choir.

Within months, our world implodes as she unravels, losing language
her laughter and singing voice trapped within her deteriorating brain.

Soon she is immobile, and one afternoon as I stand behind her wheelchair
she gazes out the front door, pointing to the sunlight, making a guttural sound.

You want to go outside? I ask, laying my hand on her shoulder. She nods.
I take her out, rolling her around until she points toward home.

She never again motions that she wants to sit in the sun.

For four months, trapped by daily dealings, caretaking devours time.
She is alive, and we exist side by side until her death.

DETRITUS

an ugly word
    litter of life
memorials of sickness reeking of death.

Educated
    clipped studied describing nothing in particular
lacking melody or soul.

I swore I would
    never use this word but it digs at my consciousness
worming its way into my mind.

Objects small treasures
    carried to California and Manhattan then home
cross continental leftovers.

Childhood's wounded prison
    rakes the fabric of time remembrances rending my heart.
Are these treasures or chains?

They've traveled my path
    shadowing stalking tripping my steps. Progress
thwarted diverted into destiny's dungeon.

Once I thought I could fly
    immortal I'd escape the inevitable stay longer than
Grandmother dead at 83 my mother at 74.

Old age my
    companion and still I carry this tidy debris. I wonder
will I leave soon or linger?

What find you
    to catalog label sell donate?
What will you keep for your journey my dear daughter?

Will you love the
　　Japanese trinkets mother's Navy locket from 1941 a time before I was?
　Or toss them to be ground to be buried in a landfill?

I am too vague
　　not sharing my secrets only leaving them as postmortem treasures
mysteries of my death.

Detritus
　　discarded interior design
meaningless but to me.

TOKENS

My Myrtle wood salad bowl sits on the counter
a gift from Kathy, my college roommate.
I sang she played piano and we performed recitals, weddings.
Naked adventures at Elysium Fields, Saturdays of bliss.
The Topanga Canyon clothes optional club is closed
and she's gone a brain aneurysm, but I have my bowl.

Aunt Frieda brought treasures from Okinawa, a kimono
and sandals with bells. Despite Mama's warning I wore
them outside, scuffing the bottoms losing their jingle.
Huarache baby shoes hang on my wall. Gifts from
Grandma Paula from Mexico, shoes and
a brightly colored child's chair.

I set my table with Oneida Twin Star stainless
a complete set Mama bought with box tops. As her
mind unraveled the teaspoons disappeared. When she
died, I found replacements on eBay of course.
My china Aunt Mary's. Royal Doulton
from the 1940s, antiques I wash by hand.

Each time I stand at my kitchen sink Daddy's
oil cans filled with fine oil for model trains greet me.
One six inches tall the other eight both with swan spouts
four times as tall as their bases. Shamrocks surround
them as they bathe in dawn's light.

To a small girl, these gifts from far off lands,
were magic and aroused my wanderlust.
They've accompanied my moves
constant reminders of the love I've shared
the shoulders upon which I stand.

NO EXIT

When this journey ends there'll be no more clothes for washing dinner to cook. No worry about which bill to pay—I'll escape my student loans—no book reviews, fretting about proper attire or messages home after this soul's shedding. We leave only love and perhaps bits and pieces of our bodies as gifts to the living. Expected or accidental, our exit lurks around a corner, a turn for which there's no round-trip ticket, no final hurrah, no do overs. When stillness comes and life's light dims, we release our bodies to Death's embrace. The roiling mind empties. After our departure, mourning echoes fill the days, then subside. Eventually the weeping of the bereft ends when they too are stilled, their lives unraveling. Only silence remains when their graves, too, are assigned. Death, the final blessing, clears paths for the birth of new souls shards of light sheared from the Source.

INEXORABLE SADNESS

Wind chatters, sweeps
ripples through branches bending
then silence.

Hours weep, rain seeps
I wake to dripping stirring
troubled thoughts.

Colors swirl my
usless fingers can not stem
the tide, flood.

Pages mock me
canvassed images fade as
life leaves.

Crows and ravens
sentinels beckoning as
Death's door closes.

DANCING DREAM

"The only dance there is."
Baba Ram Dass

This life, the only one we perceive, isn't everything, so I believe. Some scientists say our universe is a slim corner in space or one of many multiverses. Or perhaps we're living a dream? For sanity's sake, we are spared this multifaceted reality. Should I touch this apparition that tangoes in my side eye? If I did, I might be sucked into his light, landing in his dimension. Perhaps ghosts are vibrating on a different plane, not dead just in a universe where ghosts go, perhaps where humans are immortal. Papa, you're dancing in the doorway, but are you my daddy or my lover? Are you the universal phantom of fathers? We're together at Mrs. J's Sacred Cow, a trendy restaurant on the Upper West Side. But Papa, you're wearing work clothes, most inappropriate, and you're jumpin' the Big Apple, the 1937 dance craze, from before you married Mama. But the party's over and as I reach for you, you recoil. *No, baby daughter it's not your time—touching me would draw you in, rip you from the life you know.* Suddenly, I'm driving Big Blue, my 1951 Ford school bus, and I'm headed for Texas with Papa's casket in the back. Border guards stop me: *Girl is there a body in that big box?* Yep. It's my dead Daddy and I'm taking him home. Never mind that we're from Georgia, dreams will be dreams. *Girl, you can't take a dead body across state lines.* I call Texas Lady Jane, my singing buddy from Austin. We met in California where we sang country songs and I learned about Baba Ram Dass. *Jane, if you meet me, I can back up into Texas. Papa will be in Texas. Please take his coffin. The cab will still be in Arkansas, and I won't be breaking the law.* I look over my shoulder and Papa's coffin has morphed into a huge cooler of beer. I give Jane the heads up that the body is gone. I'm moving back to California. Gonna dance my life with Baba.

Christine Poythress, a daughter of the Deep South, fled to California in 1970, where she discovered Baba Ram Dass and Alan Watts. Though serious writing never crossed her mind at that time, she began journaling and scribbling poems in the margins of her drawings. While in college, she discovered opera which propelled her to New York City where she studied by day and as a singing waitress, sang arias at night. In 1983, she moved back to the South, and for 13 years, she sang country, pop, top forties, and jazz tunes in hotels, honkytonks, and corporate events. Since 2014, she has studied creative writing with award-winning author, Rosemary Daniell and has focused on writing poetry, memoir, and essays. Her work has appeared in *Quillkeepers Press, Tangled Locks Journal,* and *Synchronized Chaos.*

www.ingramcontent.com/pod-product-compliance
Lightning Source LLC
Chambersburg PA
CBHW022051080426
42734CB00009B/1299